DISGUSTING HIS

THE CRUDE, UNPLEASANT AGE OF PIRATES

THE DISGUSTING DETAILS ABOUT THE LIFE OF PIRATES

by Christopher Forest

Consultant:
Charles R. Ewen, PhD
Professor, East Carolina University
Co-editor, *X Marks the Spot: The Archaeology of Piracy*

CAPSTONE PRESS
a capstone imprint

Fact Finders is published by Capstone Press,
151 Good Counsel Drive, P.O. Box 669, Mankato, Minnesota 56002.
www.capstonepub.com

092010
005934WZS11

 Books published by Capstone Press are manufactured with paper
containing at least 10 percent post-consumer waste.

Library of Congress Cataloging-in-Publication Data
Forest, Christopher.
    The crude, unpleasant age of pirates : the disgusting details about the life of pirates / by
Christopher Forest.
        p. cm.—(Fact finders. Disgusting history)
    Summary: "Describes disgusting details about daily life on pirate ships, including housing, food,
and sanitation"—Provided by publisher.
    Includes bibliographical references and index.
    ISBN 978-1-4296-4542-3 (library binding)
    ISBN 978-1-4296-6354-0 (paperback)
    1. Pirates—Juvenile literature. I. Title. II. Series.
G535.F67 2011
910.4′5—dc22   2010002801

Editorial Credits
Katy Kudela, editor; Alison Thiele and Gene Bentdahl, designers;
    Wanda Winch, media researcher; Eric Manske, production specialist

Photo Credits
akg-images: Museum der Bildenden Künste, 9; Alamy: Lebrecht Music and Arts Photo Library, 14,
Paris Pierce, 10; The Bridgeman Art Library: ©Look and Learn/Private Collection/Peter Jackson, 18,
©Look and Learn/Private Collection/Ron Embleton, 11 (right), 27, Peter Newark Historical Pictures/Private
Collection, 16, Peter Newark Historical Pictures/Private Collection/C.T. Howard, 21, Private Collection/A.D.
McClintock, 23, Private Collection/Jean Leon Jerome Ferris, 28; iStockphoto: NoDerog, 4 (br), Stanislav
Pobytov, 4 (tl); ©National Maritime Museum, Greenwich, London, 13; Nova Development Corporation, 5
(all); Rick Reeves, Tampa, FL: cover, 7, 24: Shutterstock: akva, 14, 21 (old notebook), Andreas Meyer, 4 (bl),
Baloncici, 12, freelanceartist, grunge paper design element throughout, M.i.k.e., 8, Myotis, 20, Robb Williams,
4 (tr), Turi Tamas, banner design element throughout; www.thefruitofherhands.com/Jill Howard, 15

Primary source bibliography
Pages 14 and 21—as published in *The Buccaneers of America* by A. O. Exquemelin,
    Henry Powell, and Basil Ringrose (New York: The MacMillan Company, 1911).

TABLE OF CONTENTS

THE GOLDEN AGE OF PIRATES

1690–1725

PAGE 20

PAGE 20

PAGE 19

LEGEND

• CITY
•••• TRADE ROUTE

| 0 | 600 MI |
| 0 | 965 KM |

N
W ← → E
S

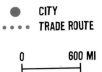

1689

William Kidd earns the name pirate; the naming of Kidd as a pirate helps usher in the Golden Age of Pirates.

1693

An earthquake destroys the city of Port Royal in Jamaica; this city was a popular pirate hideout.

PIRATE CHAIN OF COMMAND

CAPTAIN—elected by pirate crew to command the ship

FIRST MATE—helped the captain run the ship

QUARTERMASTER—handled supplies, rations, and helped keep order on the ship

PILOT—kept the ship on course

SAILOR—general crewmember

1700

Jolly Roger flags become common on pirate ships.

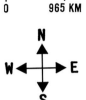

1701

England's government takes William Kidd to court for charges of being a pirate; Kidd is put to death.

1702–1713

Queen Anne's War breaks out between France and England; at the end of the war sailors are out of work, and some become pirates.

1714

New Providence in the Bahamas becomes a pirate hideout.

CAPTAIN BARTHOLOMEW ROBERTS

"No, a merry life and a short one shall be my motto."

as quoted in *Raiders and Rebels: The Golden Age of Piracy* by Frank Sherry

1716

Edward Teach joins a pirate crew; Teach later becomes known as Captain Blackbeard.

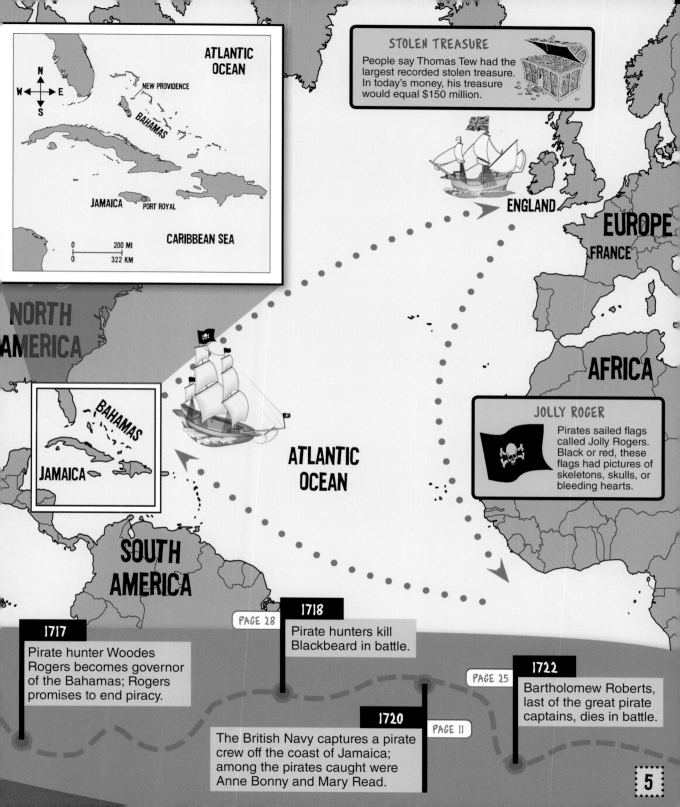

STOLEN TREASURE

People say Thomas Tew had the largest recorded stolen treasure. In today's money, his treasure would equal $150 million.

Inset map (top left)

ATLANTIC OCEAN

N W E S

NEW PROVIDENCE

BAHAMAS

JAMAICA   PORT ROYAL

CARIBBEAN SEA

0 — 200 MI
0 — 322 KM

ENGLAND

EUROPE

FRANCE

NORTH AMERICA

AFRICA

JOLLY ROGER

Pirates sailed flags called Jolly Rogers. Black or red, these flags had pictures of skeletons, skulls, or bleeding hearts.

BAHAMAS

JAMAICA

ATLANTIC OCEAN

SOUTH AMERICA

1717
Pirate hunter Woodes Rogers becomes governor of the Bahamas; Rogers promises to end piracy.

PAGE 28

1718
Pirate hunters kill Blackbeard in battle.

PAGE 25

1722
Bartholomew Roberts, last of the great pirate captains, dies in battle.

1720
The British Navy captures a pirate crew off the coast of Jamaica; among the pirates caught were Anne Bonny and Mary Read.

PAGE 11

A DEADLY CAREER

"Ahoy mate," orders a large man holding a sword. "To your post!" The smell of saltwater spray and seaweed fills the air as the large pirate ship readies to sail. Crowded onto the ship is a crew of dirty, sweaty men.

Each man moves about with a job to do. Some crewmembers struggle to pull up the ship's sails. Others blister their hands loosening ropes. Below the main deck, men move about in the dark. They stack barrels of food and water. As they work, rats scurry across the damp floor. Shouts fill the air as the ship's anchor lifts from the water. Moments later, the ship and its crew sail off on another treasure hunt.

For nearly 40 years, pirates ruled the seas. Often, pirates looked no different than people of their time. But make no mistake. These foul sailors surely did act different. Pirates made a living attacking ships, killing crews, and stealing treasure. If pirates were lucky, they lived long enough to spend their money. Unlucky pirates died at sea.

A pirate had to watch his back. Even his crewmates could turn on him.

Danger filled pirates' lives. They lost limbs in battle and suffered fatal wounds. They also endured painful and deadly diseases. But weather was the greatest danger. Storms at sea damaged ships and killed crews. A pirate's life was crude and unpleasant. Still, their rough life often paid off with stolen treasure.

LIFE AT SEA

Hundreds of pirates were often crammed on a single ship. It didn't take long before foul smells filled the air. These men shared food, beds, and toilets. The few items they brought with them were kept in common chests shared by others.

No matter how watertight the ship, water filled the lower deck. Pirates dumped out the water as fast as they could. Still, they could not rid the ship of its foul sewer smell. The decks for food storage were a bit drier. But these decks had problems too. In these dark areas, barrels and sacks of food housed worms, spiders, and rats.

Captains had private quarters, but the crew's living space was tight. Pirates found any place they could to sleep. Some chose a sack of food as a restful spot. Others found a dry place on the rough wooden floor. Fires were not allowed below deck, so pirates spent many cold, damp nights trying to keep warm. During hot weather, the stench of sweat, waste, and salt water filled the ship.

RAT

On a pirate ship, sleeping on the top deck meant fresh air.

FOUL FACT

To rid their ships of rats, pirates went hunting for the pests. A Spanish crew reported finding nearly 4,000 rats.

To make conditions even worse, pirates weren't alone below deck. Hundreds of rodents crawled over the sleeping men. Infections from rat bites sent many pirates to an early grave.

A FOUL CREW

After weeks at sea, pirates looked as foul as they smelled. Pirates had dirty hair and rotten, yellow teeth. On a pirate ship, brushing teeth and bathing rarely happened. Freshwater was saved for cooking and drinking.

Sweaty, dirty men added to the disgusting stench. Most pirates came on board a ship with only the clothes they were wearing. These clothes quickly became torn and full of bloodstains and sweat. Washing clothes helped, but pirates often only washed their shirts. A pirate's best chance at new clothes was to steal them from someone on another ship.

Picture the comfortable bathroom in your home. With one flush, waste disappears. Now picture a wooden board with some holes. That's what a pirate called a bathroom. Most pirates went to the bathroom using a simple hole in a board at the back of the ship. A pirate had to pick the right time for his bathroom stop. During rough waves, the waste sometimes fell onto the ship and onto other pirates. Yuck, watch out below!

FOUL FACT

Not all pirates were men. Anne Bonny and Mary Read dressed as men when they served aboard pirate ships.

Pirates' foul reputations matched the living quarters aboard their ships.

POOR DIET

A pirate's diet was far from fine dining. The men making meals on pirate ships were not trained cooks. These men were often crewmembers who had lost an arm or a leg in battle. They had no cooking skills and few supplies.

On a cramped ship, cooks did their best to feed hundreds of hungry men. Some ships had small kitchens. Other ships had no kitchens at all. Cooks made meals in large kettles over fires. On windy days, pirates did no cooking. One spark from a kettle fire could burn down the whole ship.

Before setting sail, pirates stocked up on vegetables and meat. But keeping food fresh was no easy task. Fresh food only lasted a few weeks. To help food last longer, cooks poured salt over vegetables and meat. As time went on, the food rotted. Cooks then used spices to hide the bad taste and served the rotten food anyway.

Wooden barrels kept food dry.

A cook on a pirate ship made meals with whatever supplies he could find.

Pirates raided towns for food and other supplies.

No Food in Sight

For these first took the leather, and sliced it in pieces. Then did they beat it between two stones, and rub it, often dipping it in the water of the river, to render it by these means supple and tender. Lastly, they scraped off the hair, and roasted or broiled it upon the fire.

Above quotation is based on the writing of Alexandre Olivier Exquemelin, as published in The Buccaneers of America, 1911.

Pirate ships sailed for weeks and months at a time. Their supplies did not last a whole voyage. Out at sea, pirates had several ways to restock their ship with food. They took food from the ships and towns they attacked. Pirates stopped at islands to hunt monkeys, birds, and turtles. They also fished for dolphins, tuna, and sea turtles.

Pirates ate a steady diet of hardtack. Made of flour and water, these hard biscuits didn't spoil as quickly as meat. Hardtack was a simple meal for ship cooks to prepare. While hardtack was easy to keep, there were still a few problems. Hardtack quickly turned stale. Tiny bugs called weevils also found their way into these biscuits. But hungry pirates didn't care. They ate the hardtack, bugs and all.

On rare occasions, pirates had no food to eat. Cooks then had to make due with whatever they could find. When supplies were low, cooks used fish bones, animal bones, and even rats to make a nasty batch of bone soup.

HARDTACK

ARMED FOR BATTLE

Pirate ships carried deadly weapons. A single pirate ship often carried up to 40 cannons. Pirates had to be skilled when firing cannons. A misfire could give a pirate frightful burns and even take off an arm or a leg.

Fear was a pirate crew's best weapon. A raised flag or a warning shot were often enough to get another ship to surrender. When these warnings didn't work, pirate captains did not think twice to order an all-out attack. Some captains even ordered "no quarter." This order meant that pirates would fight to the death.

FOUL FACT

Men who lost body parts in battle received extra money. A pirate who lost his right arm earned the most money.

Boom! During attacks, pirates fired a **volley** onto the deck of the enemy ship. Pirates wanted to hurt the crew but not the ship. The volley sprayed glass, metal, or nails across the ship's deck. Unlucky crewmembers were left bloody and even blinded.

Pirates fired warning shots.

volley: a warning shot fired from a gun or cannon

Pirates showed no mercy in battle. They would stop at nothing to get their treasure.

Painful volleys were often followed by grenades. These handmade bombs were dangerous. Once the bomb was lit, a pirate had only a matter of seconds before it blew. Pirates also threw stinkpots. They filled these clay pots with sulfur and rotten fish.

Pirates then muscled their way on ship in hand-to-hand battles. Pistols and muskets caused horrible injuries at close range. In most battles, pirates did not have much time to reload their guns. Once they fired, pirates turned their guns into clubs to strike their enemies. They also used cutlasses in close fighting. The sharp, curved edge of these swords cut deep, causing deadly wounds.

FOUL FACT

Blackbeard carried pistols, knives, and two swords with him at all times. He was one of the most feared pirates of the golden age.

PIRATE TREASURE

Pirates were willing to suffer disease, foul food, and deadly battles for one thing—treasure! Pirates captured ships and took their prized **booty**. In a pirate's world, almost anything was treasure. Pirates sold cloth, spices, and supplies for money. They even sold slaves. From anchors to rope, pirates stripped ships clean. Sometimes they even took the whole ship.

Beware! No one was safe when pirates went looking for treasure. Pirate crews sometimes held prisoners and whole towns for **ransom**. Pirates like Blackbeard showed no kindness. Stories say Blackbeard sliced off a man's finger just to get the man's diamond ring.

What did pirates do with their treasure? Few pirates, if any, buried their treasure. Most pirates sailed to hideouts. Port Royal, Jamaica, and New Providence in the Bahamas were favorite stops. Pirates felt at home in these wild ports. But they soon lost their money playing cards and dice.

booty: stolen goods

ransom: money that is demanded before someone or something will be set free

Pirates divided their treasure once they made it to shore.

Not All Gold and Riches

The ship being taken, they found none in her what they thought … All the treasure they got consisted only in fifty bars of iron, a small parcel of paper, some earthen jars full of wine, and other things of this kind; all of small importance.

Above quotation is based on the writing of Alexandre Olivier Exquemelin, as published in The Buccaneers of America, 1911.

BETTER NOT GET SICK!

Pirates had treasure, but what they really needed were doctors. On a pirate ship, a cook or carpenter became the ship doctor. These sailors had no medical training. They were chosen because they had a knife or saw. As ship doctors, they needed these tools to cut off injured arms and legs.

During battles, pirates suffered many injuries. With little medicine or clean water, wounds became infected. Arms and legs that did not heal were **amputated**. Often, the ship doctor had to cut off the limb within 24 hours of the injury. A doctor used a red-hot saw or knife to remove the limb. The doctor hoped the heat of the knife or saw would stop the bleeding. If so, a pirate just might live. Of course, a pirate had to first make it through all the pain. There was no medicine, so pirates were awake through the entire operation.

amputate: to cut off someone's arm, leg, or other body part

FOUL FACT

Pirates who lost hands or legs often wore peg legs and hooks. Pirates made these tools from materials found on their ships.

On dirty ships, diseases spread quickly. Dysentery and smallpox wiped out pirate crews. Many more pirates suffered from scurvy. This painful disease gave pirates loose teeth, rotten gums, and bleeding under the skin. If left untreated, patients died. To stop scurvy, pirates drank ale with herbs. Later they learned to eat citrus fruit to prevent the disease.

On a pirate ship, many battle wounds turned deadly.

After many days at sea, tempers flared and fights broke out.

PIRATE CODES

After months at sea, pirates grew restless and often fought each other or their captain. It wasn't easy for a captain to keep order over a crew of men. Pirates were stuck together for many days. These hot, tired men often lashed out at each other.

Most pirate captains kept control by using fear and harsh punishments. Pirate codes helped captains run their ships. These codes were a strict set of rules pirates had to follow.

One of the most famous set of pirate codes was created by Bartholomew "Black Bart" Roberts. This fierce captain ruled a tight ship. His men could not gamble. Candles had to be put out at 8:00 each night. Pirates aboard Black Bart's ship had to follow the codes or risk injury and even death.

No matter the codes, each pirate captain had one idea in mind—controlling the ship. A captain's worst fear was **mutiny**. During a mutiny, unhappy pirates tried to rid a ship of its captain and his loyal crew. Some angry crews killed their captains. Others sent their captains out to sea in small boats with no food or water.

mutiny: a revolt against the captain of a ship

KEEPING ORDER

Life on a pirate ship was clear-cut. Pirates who followed the rules and fought in battles received rewards. Pirates who broke the rules faced terrible punishments.

On a pirate ship, even minor crimes had painful punishments. A pirate who took a lit candle below deck was **flogged**. The guilty pirate was whipped only once on the back. Left with a scar, the pirate would never forget this punishment.

A repeated crime or a serious crime could lead to keelhauling. For this punishment, a ship's crew tied a pirate to a rope. They lowered him into the water and dragged him under the ship. Sharp barnacles shredded the pirate's skin. His lungs quickly filled with water. Keelhauling was almost always deadly.

What's a punishment worse than death? Being **marooned**. An angry captain marooned a pirate on an island. These islands were often just sandbars, reefs, or stretches of empty land with no food or freshwater. The marooned pirate was given a bottle of water or rum and a pistol loaded with a single shot. Pirates could use the pistol to end their suffering. But many marooned pirates slowly starved to death. Others were swept away by the ocean tides.

Few marooned pirates lived to tell their story.

flog: to be whipped by a special whip called a cat-o'-nine tails

maroon: to be left alone on a deserted island

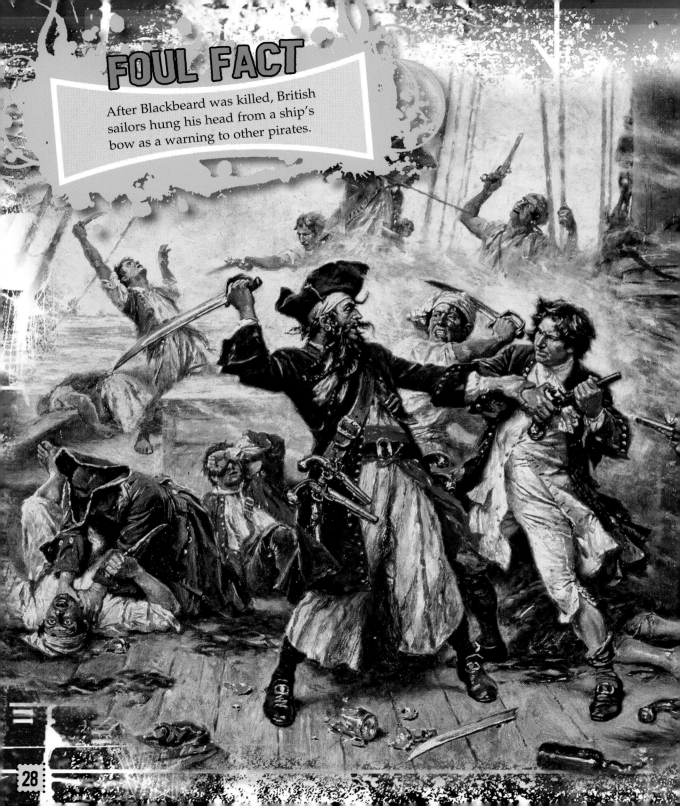

FOUL FACT

After Blackbeard was killed, British sailors hung his head from a ship's bow as a warning to other pirates.

GOLDEN AGE ENDS

During the golden age, pirates sailed the seas risking disease and death for treasure. But by the 1720s, their days were numbered. Navies around the world began to fight back against pirates.

Pirate hunters chased and captured pirates. At sea, navies attacked and destroyed pirate ships.

Captured pirates were quickly tried and hanged for their crimes. Town officials hung pirate bodies in ship harbors. These rotting bodies were a grim warning for pirates hoping to come ashore.

By the early 1800s, the life of pirates had changed. The pirates who once ruled the seas were now just outlaws on the run. They were no longer fierce hunters. Instead, pirates had become the hunted. Their captures and deaths brought an end to their golden age.

Even the feared pirate Blackbeard was killed by pirate hunters.

GLOSSARY

amputate (AM-pyuh-tayt)—to cut off someone's arm, leg, or other body part, usually because the part is damaged

barnacle (BAR-nuh-kuhl)—a small shellfish that attaches itself firmly to the sides of boats, rocks, and other shellfish

booty (BOO-tee)—money or goods taken in a war or robbery

deck (DEK)—the floor of a boat or a ship

dysentery (DI-sen-tayr-ee)—a serious infection of the intestines

flog (FLOG)—to be whipped by a special whip called a cat-o'-nine tails

maroon (muh-ROON)—to be left alone on a deserted island

musket (MUHSS-kit)—a gun with a long barrel that was used before the rifle was invented

mutiny (MYOOT-uh-nee)—a revolt against the captain of a ship

ransom (RAN-suhm)—money that is demanded before someone or something will be set free

scurvy (SKUR-vee)—a deadly disease caused by lack of vitamin C

sulfur (SUHL-fur)—a yellow chemical element used in gunpowder

volley (VOL-ee)—a gun or cannon shot fired, often as a warning

READ MORE

Mattern, Joanne. *Pirates*. Warriors Graphic Illustrated. Vero Beach, Fla.: Rourke Pub., 2010.

O'Donnell, Liam. *The Pirate Code: Life of a Pirate*. The Real World of Pirates. Mankato, Minn.: Capstone Press, 2007.

Price, Sean Stewart. *Pirates: Truth and Rumors*. Truth and Rumors. Mankato, Minn.: Capstone Press, 2011.

Yolen, Jane. *Sea Queens: Women Pirates Around the World*. Watertown, Mass.: Charlesbridge, 2008.

INTERNET SITES

FactHound offers a safe, fun way to find Internet sites related to this book. All of the sites on FactHound have been researched by our staff.

Here's all you do:

Visit *www.facthound.com*

Type in this code: 9781429645423

INDEX